You Should Be Writing

You Should Be Writing

A Journal of Inspiration & Instruction to Keep Your Pen Moving

by

Brenda Knight & Nita Sweeney

CORAL GABLES

Published by Mango Publishing Group, a division of Mango Media Inc.

Cover Design, Layout & Design: Morgane Leoni
Cover Photo: © Panudda/shutterstock.com
Interior Illustration: © castecodesign/stock.adobe.com

For permission requests, please contact the publisher at:
Mango Publishing Group
2850 S Douglas Road, 2nd Floor
Coral Gables, FL 33134 USA
info@mango.bz

For special orders, quantity sales, course adoptions and corporate sales, please email the publisher at sales@mango.bz. For trade and wholesale sales, please contact Ingram Publisher Services at customer.service@ingramcontent.com or +1.800.509.4887.

You Should Be Writing: A Journal of Inspiration & Instruction to Keep Your Pen Moving

Library of Congress Cataloging-in-Publication number: 2020933927
ISBN: (print) 978-1-64250-255-8, (ebook) 978-1-64250-256-5
BISAC category code SEL009000, SELF-HELP / Creativity

Printed in the United States of America

In loving memory of Rich Chin

Contents

Foreword

YOUR PEN IS MIGHTIER

As an author, I have heard of and experienced truly frightening writerly maladies: page blindness, *horror vacui* (otherwise known as fear of the blank space), creative paralysis, inner critic overload, and, of course, the old standby—writer's block. As a writer, I too have experienced many of these phases, the worst being muse abandonment.

How do word wranglers deal with this?

Proust took to his bed but, thankfully, nibbled madeleines dipped in lime tea, and thus *Remembrance of Things Past* poured forth. Voltaire drank as many as thirty to fifty cups of coffee a day, which surely must have left no time to tend his own garden. Female scribes including brilliants Marguerite Duras, Patricia Highsmith, Elizabeth Bishop, Jane Bowles, Anne Sexton, Carson McCullers, Dorothy Parker, and Shirley Jackson were known to imbibe as well.

Franz Kafka once complained, "How time flies; another ten days and I have achieved nothing. It doesn't come off. A page now and then is successful, but I can't keep it up; the next day I am powerless."

I subscribe to the Jack London school of daily effort. London believed that writing daily was the best way to rouse the sleeping Muse. He advised, "Set yourself a 'stint,' and see that you do that 'stint' each day; you will have more words to your credit at the end of the year."

I also agree wholeheartedly with Maya Angelou to just keep at it. "The trick is not to overthink it. Write nonsense if you have to. But keep writing, no matter if you're pleased with the final result or not."

Toni Morrison believed in establishing a ritual for your writing time—be it music, coffee, a certain time of day or whatever works for you.

Stephen King offered a cautionary tale about the perils of writer's block with his memorable novel, *The Shining*. And, this much is true, all work and no play makes any of us quite dull.

But do not despair. Before you pick up your axe or start talking to ghosts, try a more spirited approach to getting inspired and journal. Or doodle, make lists, or jot down your dreams.

Hillary Mantel, author of *Wolf Hall*, among her excellent works, may well offer the most helpful advice of all.

> If you get stuck, get away from your desk. Take a walk, take a bath, go to sleep, make a pie, draw, listen to music, meditate, exercise; whatever you do, don't just stick there scowling at the problem. But don't make telephone calls

or go to a party; if you do, other people's words will pour in where your lost words should be. Open a gap for them, create a space. Be patient.

This journal is intended to be a place for you to get away and explore the outer reaches of your immense imagination.

It may also help to remember the immense power of writing. A writer's great gift is the ability to transmogrify experience even as a host becomes the Body of Christ, if you will indulge my Irish Catholic sensibilities for a moment.

One can uplift, inspire, console, and commune with one's words, or one can denigrate, depress, alarm, or alienate. I choose my words carefully and try to be an apprentice of the first way. It's easier to do in writing because one has time to think before blurting out some unkind missive.

As my sophomore year journalism teacher, Sister Michael David, BVM, once told her eager students, "Choose your words carefully; they are a matter of life and death." She then proved her point by telling us that when Queen Victoria wanted to quell a revolution in Ireland, she rounded up all the poets and writers and hung them—that's how powerful one's words can be to the world.

Warmly,
BECCA ANDERSON

Introduction

TEN MINUTES, GO!

"You should be writing."

It echoes in your head as you circle the desk, go for a run, watch a movie, pet the dog, eat dinner, have sex, do your best to fall asleep. You might not know why you're not writing. Even if you did, it probably wouldn't help.

You're not alone. At some point, nearly every writer (including yours truly) struggles with the inability to get (or keep) the pen moving. Unfortunately, that fact won't help either. You might feel less lonely, but it won't fill the page.

The only cure for not writing is writing. That's where this journal comes in.

You should be writing.

Let this journal be a space for you to start, get lost, finish, abandon, return to, and simply have. Let this be a place where your pen flows freely and you get your words down while your head is filled with inspiring and instructive quotes from some of the world's best writers.

Start this journal at the beginning and work your way through, or open to any page, find a quote that feeds you, use that as your prompt, and GO! Just get your pen moving. That's the key. We are fighting inertia, apathy, and terror. The remedy for each is the same. Get your pen moving and let the words lead.

If you're a thinking type, make your outlines on these pages. Sketch your characters. Plan your story. Draw your maps and battlefields. Design the clothing and makeup. Plot your grand schemes.

Heart-centered writers might doodle or make lists of all the people their writing will help or change. Pour your huge heart onto the page. Just get moving.

At each of the twenty-five week-long writing retreats I attended or assisted with bestselling author Natalie Goldberg, when it was time to write, her cue was always the same. "Ten minutes, **GO!**" The only thing more powerful than the pen is the timer. Whether I use the microwave timer, the white digital model I keep in my backpack, or the app on my phone, the pressure cooker effect of setting a specified amount of writing time saves me again and again. It's only ten minutes. I can do nearly anything (endure nearly any pain) for ten minutes. Once I get going, the timer goes off, and I ignore it. The water is flowing. I'm free. Try that if it helps you begin. Just, begin!

It's been a joy to gather and organize theses quotes. Brenda and I eagerly piled up our favorites, and I divided them into chapters that made sense to me. The quotes on the left-hand pages are intended to inspire, while those on the right-hand pages instruct. Brenda and I did our best to cover all the bases, but you surely have more of your own.

So, use this journal in whatever way suits you. But please, get to it.

At Natalie's retreats, we chanted this reminder:

> I beg to urge you everyone:
> Life and Death are a Great Matter
> Awaken, awaken, awaken
> Time passes quickly
> Do not waste this precious life.

Now, **GO!**

Chapter 1

WRITING TIPS FROM THE GREATS

Every vocation has a long history of apprenticeship. Writing is no different. We writers can learn from the hard-earned experience of the masters, studying techniques honed from years of practice and success. We can watch, take their work apart, learn their habits, and mimic them in order to find our way. We can follow the trail of breadcrumbs they left behind and see if it suits our work.

You have to simply love writing, and you have to remind yourself often that you love it.

—Susan Orlean

Leave a decent space of time between writing something and
editing it.

—Zadie Smith

An artist must be free to choose what he does, certainly, but he must also never be afraid to do what he might choose.

—Langston Hughes

Sometimes, you don't know which ideas are the good ones until you try them. I will give anything a try, and you can kind of tell when you're writing something that's not working.

—Veronica Roth

_____

_____

_____

_____

_____

_____

_____

_____

_____

_____

_____

_____

_____

_____

_____

_____

_____

_____

_____

_____

_____

_____

_____

As a writer, a failure is just information. It's something that I've done wrong in writing, or is inaccurate or unclear. I recognize failure—which is important; some people don't—and fix it.

—Toni Morrison

You have to strip yourself of all your disguises, some of which you didn't know you had. You want to write a sentence as clean as a bone. That is the goal.

—James Baldwin

A lot of my best decisions were made in a state of self-delusion. When you're trying to create a career as a writer, a little delusional thinking goes a long way.

—Michael Lewis

_____

_____

_____

_____

_____

_____

_____

_____

_____

_____

_____

_____

_____

_____

_____

_____

_____

_____

_____

_____

Forget the books you want to write. Think only of the book you
are writing.

—Henry Miller

For those whose bucket list includes seeing their name on the spine of a book, it boils down to the power of persistence. Write on.

—Marlene Wagman-Geller

Finish the day's writing when you still want to continue.

—Helen Dunmore

I wish somebody had told me that I could slow down and take [writing] at my own pace. If you feel like you're getting "left behind" ... take as much time as you need.

—Danez Smith

I myself find that I trust my own writing most, and others seem to trust it most, too, when I sound most like a person from Indianapolis, which is what I am.

—Kurt Vonnegut

> Once I started doing it, I couldn't imagine wanting to do anything else for a living. I noticed very quickly that writing was the only way for me to lose track of the time.
>
> **—Michael Lewis**

Protect the time and space in which you write. Keep everybody away from it, even the people who are most important to you.

—Zadie Smith

The cutting of the gem has to be finished before you can see whether it shines.

—Leonard Cohen

When I was twenty-one, my first editor said that my intuition would take me further than my education ever would... I could put on a page that what felt good to me.

—Jason Reynolds

_____

_____

_____

_____

_____

_____

_____

_____

_____

_____

_____

_____

_____

_____

_____

_____

_____

_____

_____

_____

_____

_____

_____

_____

Nobody can tell you how to start writing. The only good reason for writing is that one has to write.

—T.S. Eliot

Chapter 2

Accessing Your Well
of Creativity

We each have a well of creativity. It might be buried beneath years of self-doubt, criticism from others, or societal conventions. It might have run dry and need to be refilled. The quotes in this section will help you discover, replenish, and maintain this essential asset and plumb the depths already within.

Process over product. This simple mantra nudges me back to the page when my efficiency-crazed mind resists writing for fear of wasting my time.

—Pat Snyder

A pen works best when the ink flows freely. A writer works best when the spirit flows freely. Learn and practice some form of deep relaxation—even five centering breaths—and feel the spigot open.

—Brenda Knight

_____

_____

_____

_____

_____

_____

_____

_____

_____

_____

_____

_____

_____

_____

_____

_____

_____

_____

_____

_____

_____

_____

_____

_____

The way a writer grows is just as mysterious as the way an apple tree grows. But given the right nourishment our work will continue to ripen, until one day we're ready, and the fruit will fall.

—Sean W. Murphy

Never stop when you are stuck. You may not be able to solve the problem, but turn aside and write something else. Do not stop altogether.

—Jeanette Winterson

In both writing and sleeping, we learn to be physically still at the same time we are encouraging our minds to unlock from the humdrum rational thinking of our daytime lives.

—Stephen King

A problem with a piece of writing often clarifies itself if you go for a long walk.

—Helen Dunmore

Moments of pure inspiration are glorious, but most of a writer's life is, to adapt the old cliché, about perspiration rather than inspiration. Sometimes you have to write even when the muse isn't cooperating.

—J.K. Rowling

Writing is a lot like making soup. My subconscious cooks the idea,
but I have to sit down at the computer to pour it out.

—Robin Wells

There are two of you—one who wants to write and one who doesn't. The one who wants to write better keep tricking the one who doesn't.

—Maria Irene Fornes

If you write what you yourself sincerely think and feel and are interested in, the chances are very high that you will interest other people as well.

—**Rachel Carson**

Breakthroughs [in writing] come from putting an inordinate amount of pressure on yourself and seeing what you can take, and hoping that you grow some new muscles.

—Ta-Nehisi Coates

Turn up for work. Discipline allows creative freedom. No discipline equals no freedom.

—Jeanette Winterson

One can never be alone enough to write. To see better.

—Susan Sontag

I never consciously set out to write a certain story. The idea must originate somewhere deep within me and push itself out in its own time. Usually, it begins with associations.

—Ray Bradbury

I imagine I am obsessed with the person, thing, or place I'm writing about. Then, like being on an exhilarating first date, I notice every detail and nuance and fill the page.

—Lisa Haneberg

When writers procrastinate, it's often because of perfectionism. Free yourself from your "I must be perfect" expectations. Plunge in, and allow yourself to be beautifully, humanly, creatively, wonderfully imperfect!

—Tania Casselle

If you live with dogs, you'll never run out of things to write about.

—Sharon Delarose

_____

_____

_____

_____

_____

_____

_____

_____

_____

_____

_____

_____

_____

_____

_____

_____

_____

_____

_____

_____

_____

_____

_____

Chapter 3

THE ART OF STORYTELLING

It's one thing to write well and another to tell a story. Powerful writing requires both. A good story captures the listener or, in the case of the written word, the reader. How many of us have been rapt by a good storyteller's skill at spinning a yarn? These authors provide tips to help us learn this essential skill.

A story should be like a river, flowing and never stopping, your readers, passengers on a boat whirling downstream through constantly refreshing and changing scenery.

—Ray Bradbury

When you get to a dramatic moment, you slice it. You slow it down, so you get the full dramatic impact of it.

—Bryan Smith

Story is the umbilical cord that connects us to the past, present, and future. Family. Story is a relationship between the teller and the listener, a responsibility. Story is an affirmation of our ties to one another.

—Terry Tempest Williams

A character is a caricature. If a writer can make people live, there may be no great characters in his book.

—Ernest Hemingway

_____
_____
_____
_____
_____
_____
_____
_____
_____
_____
_____
_____
_____
_____
_____
_____
_____
_____
_____
_____
_____
_____
_____
_____
_____

Nobody's life is tied up in a bow. Stories that end in a bow are kind of disrespectful to the reader. If you want your story to be compelling, let it fade to black without reconciliation.

—Jason Reynolds

A short story must have single mood and every sentence must build towards it.

—Edgar Allen Poe

Storytelling, like rhetoric...answers both our curiosity and our longing for shapely forms: our profound desire to know what happens and our persistent hope that what happens will somehow make sense.

—Jane Hirshfield

In writing, your audience is one single reader. I have found that sometimes it helps to pick out one person—a real person you know, or an imagined person and write to that one.

—John Steinbeck

You're never going to kill storytelling because it's built into the human plan. We come with it.

—**Margaret Atwood**

Use the time of a total stranger in such a way that he or she will not feel the time was wasted.

—Kurt Vonnegut

A story has no beginning or end: arbitrarily one chooses that moment of experience from which to look back or from which to look ahead.

—Graham Greene

In many cases when a reader puts a story aside because it "got boring," the boredom arose because the writer grew enchanted with his powers of description and lost sight of his priority, which is to keep the ball rolling.

—Stephen King

We tell ourselves stories in order to live.

—Joan Didion

> Every character should want something, even if it is only a glass of water.

—Kurt Vonnegut

I am a good listener and a story hunter. Everybody has a story and all stories are interesting if they are told in the right tone.

—Isabel Allende

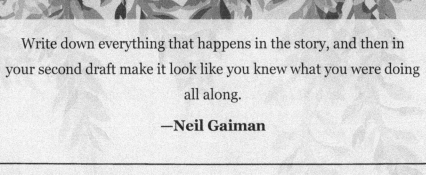

Write down everything that happens in the story, and then in your second draft make it look like you knew what you were doing all along.

—Neil Gaiman

I'm much more interested in character and the texture of setting than I am in what happens next, which only exists so that they'll have something to react to, which defines them.

—Rosellen Brown

Chapter 4

THE CRAFT OF WRITING

Every writer wants to know how to write well. But what does it mean and how do we do it? The skill set includes grammar, punctuation, sentence structure, and word choice, but there's another essence a good writer must learn—craft. The quotes in this chapter will help you practice your craft.

Writing is 10 percent about writing first drafts and 90 percent about editing. If you feel like inspiration is hard to come by, that means you get to focus on the things you already have.

—Danez Smith

Any writing project has a life of its own. You might think you know what a piece will be about, but beyond those fixed ideas there are often much richer jewels if you dare to trust the process, let go of control, and discover what is waiting to be born in you.

—Tania Casselle

Secure writers don't sell first drafts. They patiently rewrite until the script is as director-ready, as actor-ready as possible. Unfinished work invites tampering, while polished, mature work seals its integrity.

—Robert McKee

It's worth the work to find the precise word that will create a feeling or describe a situation. Use a thesaurus, use your imagination...but find the right word.

—Isabel Allende

A book is never, ever finished. You simply get to a point where you and your editor are reasonably happy with how it is and you go with that. Left to our own devices, a writer would endlessly fiddle with a book, changing little thing after little thing.

—Kimberly Pauley

To shift the structure of a sentence alters the meaning of that sentence, as definitely and inflexibly as the position of a camera alters the meaning of the object photographed.

—Joan Didion

Fiction does not spring into the world fully grown, like Athena. It is the process of writing and rewriting that makes a fiction original, if not profound.

—John Gardner

You can't just describe something. The details you provide have to bear on the story, to foreshadow, or amplify or create the mood.

—Bryan Smith

_____

_____

_____

_____

_____

_____

_____

_____

_____

_____

_____

_____

_____

_____

_____

_____

_____

_____

_____

_____

_____

_____

_____

Why should you examine your writing style with the idea of improving it? If you scribble your thoughts any which way, your reader will surely feel that you care nothing about them.

—Kurt Vonnegut

_____
_____
_____
_____
_____
_____
_____
_____
_____
_____
_____
_____
_____
_____
_____
_____
_____
_____
_____
_____
_____
_____

I did not begin with craft, I began with strong feelings and worked toward craft.

—**Dorothy Allison**

Most writers don't talk about their craft—they just do it.

—Alfred Lansing

Every sentence has a purpose. It doesn't exist to take up space, it exists to change the reader, to move her from here to there. This sentence, then, what's it for? If it doesn't move us closer to where we seek to go, delete it.

—Seth Godin

The Book is more important than your plans for it. You have to go with what works for The Book—if your ideas appear hollow or forced when they are put on paper, chop them, erase them, pulverize them and start again. Don't whine when things are not going your way, because they are going the right way for The Book, which is more important. The show must go on, and so must The Book.

—E.A. Bucchianeri

Fortune for Writers: If you live up north, write about the sun in the south. If you live down south, write about the cold in the north. If you are nowhere, write about a somewhere. Discover empathy in the process. Lucky number: 1,000,000,000.

—Ira Sukrungruang

When worrying about how much detail you need to include in your memoir writing, remember to pack light. Success in writing always involves hard choices on what to leave out. Just because something happened doesn't make it interesting. What makes any detail interesting is if it drives your story forward.

—Marion Roach Smith

Art stands on the shoulders of craft, which means that to get to the art, you must master the craft. If you want to write, practice writing.

—Ann Patchett

Why do we write? A chorus erupts. Because we cannot simply live.

—Patti Smith

Chapter 5

READ YOUR WAY IN

What better way to learn to write than to study the writings of other authors? Most writers began reading young and wanted to be the one with their name on the spine of a book. Many writers remember that feeling of being so lost in a story that they missed the dinner bell and a parent had to call repeatedly to bring them to supper. The book was food enough.

As writers practicing our craft, the joy of reading gives way to the need to take a book apart and figure out how it's done. Why the line break there? How did she weave in the backstory? What made the character come to life? We read not only for pleasure, but to steal and learn. The ecstasy in uncovering that magic is the best mystery of all.

Breathing book molecules helps you write. It's a fact.

—Ame Dyckman

You can't be a good writer without being a devoted reader. Reading is the best way of analyzing what makes a good book. Notice what works and what doesn't, what you enjoyed and why.

—J.K. Rowling

The answers to our questions, both technical and artistic, lie
between the pages written by those who have gone before us. Read.

—Nat Russo

Make your mentors the people on your bookshelf, the people you look up to. I consider James Baldwin to be a very big mentor of mine. James Baldwin has been not alive my entire life.

—Danez Smith

The love of books. My library is an archive of longings.

—Susan Sontag

Read at the level at which you want to write. Reading is the
nourishment that feeds the kind of writing you want to do.

—Jennifer Egan

> If you only read the books that everyone else is reading, you can only think what everyone else is thinking.
>
> **—Haruki Murakami**

Develop craftsmanship through years of wide reading.

—Annie Proulx

What I didn't realize at first is that besides being destined to be a reader, I was also destined to be a writer, and I don't think one is less important than the other.

—Jorge Luis Borges

Find an author you admire (mine was Conrad) and copy their plots and characters in order to tell your own story, just as people learn to draw and paint by copying the masters.

—Michael Moorcock

Five common traits of good writers:

1. They have something to say.

2. They read widely and have done so since childhood.

3. They possess what Isaac Asimov calls a "capacity for clear thought," able to go from point to point in an orderly sequence, an A to Z approach.

4. They're geniuses at putting their emotions into words.

5. They possess an insatiable curiosity, constantly asking Why and How.

—James J. Kilpatrick

I learned from the age of two or three that any room in our house, at any time of day, was there to read in, or be read to.

—Eudora Welty

A bookstore is one of the only pieces of evidence we have that people are still thinking.

—Jerry Seinfeld

Read a lot. But read as a writer, to see how other writers are doing it. And make your knowledge of literature in English as deep and broad as you can. In workshops, writers are often told to read what is being written now, but if that is all you read, you are limiting yourself. You need to get a good overall sense of English literary history, so you can write out of that knowledge.

—Theodora Goss

No aspiring author should content himself with a mere acquisition of technical rules... All attempts at gaining literary polish must begin with judicious reading.

—**H.P. Lovecraft**

Read. Read at least a hundred books in the genre in which you want to write to get a sense for how things work—or not—in that style of writing. If you write for children, try to do some of that reading out loud.

—Kate Messner

You will learn more about writing from one hour of reading than you will in six hours of writing.

—John McAleer

Chapter 6

Waxing Poetic

Another element of writing, beyond content and meaning, is the shape and form and sound and rhythm of words and sentences. We choose words not just for meaning, but for ebb and flow. The quotes in this section offer assistance, primarily from the poets, to help writers listen to their writing. If you're not already reading your work out loud, this section will remind you why the shape and sound of words can convey as much meaning as the choice of a word itself.

Breathe in experience, breathe out poetry.

—Muriel Rukeyser

Lines of good poetry are apt to be a little irregular. A prevailing sense of rhythm is necessary, but some variation enhances the very strength of the pattern. The singsong poem is a dull poem.

—Mary Oliver

Is poetry language that is spontaneous, impulsive? Yes, it is. Is it also language that is composed, considered, appropriate, and effective, though you read the poem a hundred times? Yes, it is.

—Alice Walker

You have to be honest. You have to choose words that breathe. It doesn't have to necessarily be correct English, but you need words with life.

—Jason Reynolds

_____

_____

_____

_____

_____

_____

_____

_____

_____

_____

_____

_____

_____

_____

_____

_____

_____

_____

_____

_____

_____

_____

Something that you feel will find its own form.

—Jack Kerouac

There's only one way a poet can develop his actual writing—apart from self-criticism & continual practice. And that is by reading other poetry aloud. What matters, above all, is educating the ear.

—T.S. Eliot

For me the best time is at the end of the day, when you've written and forgotten. You wrote longer than you expected to. You've been so absorbed in it that it got late.

—Mary Karr

_____

_____

_____

_____

_____

_____

_____

_____

_____

_____

_____

_____

_____

_____

_____

_____

_____

_____

_____

_____

_____

Every good piece of writing begins with both a mystery and a love story. And that every single sentence must be a poem. And that economy is the key to all good writing. And that every character has to have a secret.

—Silas House

The poet's voice need not merely be the record of man, it can be one of the props, the pillars to help him endure and prevail.

—William Faulkner

Writing is not an exercise in excision, it's a journey into sound.

—E.B. White

Writing is a visual art.

—Natalie Goldberg

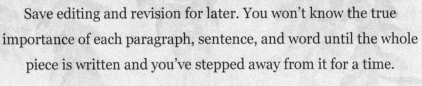

Save editing and revision for later. You won't know the true importance of each paragraph, sentence, and word until the whole piece is written and you've stepped away from it for a time.

—Lisa Haneberg

_____

_____

_____

_____

_____

_____

_____

_____

_____

_____

_____

_____

_____

_____

_____

_____

_____

_____

_____

_____

_____

_____

_____

_____

Making a poem is neither a wholly conscious activity nor an act of unconscious transcription—it is a way for new thinking and feeling to come into existence.

—Jane Hirshfield

No iron can pierce the human heart as chillingly as a full stop placed at the right time.

—Isaac Babel

Poetry is vague affirmation and bewildering clarification. Like the most poignant of emotions, we understand the essence but cannot adequately do it verbal justice, crippled by inherently weak tongues.

—Richelle E. Goodrich

Fill your papers with the breathings of your heart.

—William Wadsworth

Poetry should be like a crystal: it should make life more beautiful and less real.

—Oscar Wilde

Chapter 7

Drawing Influence from Other Works of Art

Every form of art can provide sustenance to writers. Be open to it all. Look around. Take it in. See it. Let it feed you, inspire you, and shape your work. Let it fill your creative well and move you to share your stories on the page.

Life isn't a support system for art. It's the other way around.

—Stephen King

In poetry we pare down our thoughts into their most graceful shapes, like minimalist sculptures.

—Patricia Robin Woodruff

What can an art of words take from the art that needs none? Yet I often think I've learned as much from watching dancers as I have from reading.

—Zadie Smith

_____
_____
_____
_____
_____
_____
_____
_____
_____
_____
_____
_____
_____
_____
_____
_____
_____
_____
_____
_____
_____
_____
_____

Learn the rules like a pro so you can break them like an artist.

—Pablo Picasso

Music was my refuge. I could crawl into the space between the notes and curl my back to loneliness.

—Maya Angelou

Don't be afraid to scrape the paint off and do it again. This is the way you learn, trial and error, over and over, repetition. It pays you great dividends, great, great dividends.

—**Bob Ross**

You must forget all your theories, all your ideas before the subject.
What part of these is really your own will be expressed in your
expression of the emotion awakened in you by the subject.

—Henri Matisse

Be aware of wonder. Live a balanced life—learn some and think some and draw and paint and sing and dance and play and work every day some.

—Robert Fulghum

When you step from the wings onto the stage you go from total blackness to a blinding hot glare. After a moment you adjust, but there is that moment. like being inside lightning.

—Meg Howrey

_____

_____

_____

_____

_____

_____

_____

_____

_____

_____

_____

_____

_____

_____

_____

_____

_____

_____

_____

_____

_____

We're breaking all the rules. Even our own rules. And how do we do that? By leaving plenty of room for X quantities.

—John Cage

A writer, to be connected to the world, should have a circle that cares about the world. And out of that would come the writing.

—Alice Walker

_____
_____
_____
_____
_____
_____
_____
_____
_____
_____
_____
_____
_____
_____
_____
_____
_____
_____
_____
_____
_____
_____
_____
_____

I should have danced more when I had no fear of falling.

—Kim Cormack

A fine work of art—music, dance, painting, story—has the power to silence the chatter in the mind and lift us to another place.

—Robert McKee

One ought, every day at least, to hear a little song, read a good poem, see a fine picture, and, if it were possible, to speak a few reasonable words.

—Johann Wolfgang von Goethe

Everything I see or do, the weather and the water, buildings... everything actual is an advantage when I am writing. It is like a menu...and I can pick and choose what I want.

—Toni Morrison

_____
_____
_____
_____
_____
_____
_____
_____
_____
_____
_____
_____
_____
_____
_____
_____
_____
_____
_____
_____
_____
_____
_____
_____

I was afraid of the dance once, too. But I learned to embrace it and the mistakes I would make. Do not turn away from your fear. Turn toward love instead.

—Holly Lynn Payne

The key to understanding any people is in its art: its writing, painting, sculpture.

—Louis L'Amour

Chapter 8

WRITING AS MEDICINE

Poultice. Salve. Healer. Binding agent. Bandage. Translator. Muse.

The quotes in this section reflect the powerful impact of writing on the author. We've each heard the suggestion "Put your own oxygen mask on first." Sometimes writing helps you breathe, keeps you alive.

Especially in first drafts, we often write solely for ourselves. There is no audience beyond the small and possibly wounded child who sings (or screams) from the depths of our being. This writing may never leave our notebooks. Or, in revision, it may transform into powerful prose to which an audience can relate. No matter the end result, writing heals.

When the writing's going well, I feel fueled by a hidden source. During those times it doesn't matter if things are going wrong in my life; I have this alternate energy source that's active.

—Jennifer Egan

_____
_____
_____
_____
_____
_____
_____
_____
_____
_____
_____
_____
_____
_____
_____
_____
_____
_____
_____
_____
_____

He began to write his thoughts and observations concerning the day's events. It helped him better understand everything he had seen and done over the course of the day.

—Christopher Paolini

Writing practice infuses my spirit with a vitality that had been lacking. I think of it as a thriving connection with the deep unconscious self that is so generative to the psyche/spirit.

—Philip Kenney

If you take some time to write out how you're feeling, it can help you relinquish the attachment to ruminating over what was said or done. Writing down how you feel provides an opportunity for you to be honest with yourself. It provides a safe and private space to reveal something to yourself that you may not be ready to reveal to someone else.

—Bridgitte Jackson-Buckley

Writing is not just a process of creation. It is also a process of self-discovery.

—Cristina Istrati

Nothing so sharpens the thought process as writing down one's arguments. Weaknesses overlooked in oral discussion become painfully obvious on the written page.

—Hyman G. Rickover

But I have long loved the written word, and come to see in it the power of the sleeping lion. This is my name. This is who I am. This is how I got here. In the absence of an audience, I will write down my story so that it waits like a restful beast with lungs breathing and heart beating.

—Lawrence Hill

Be thankful for the people who have stood by you and cheered you on, but don't forget to be thankful for the ones that said it could not be done. Writing a book is no small task and even the skeptics can help you get where you want to be!

—CK Webb

There is something about just setting the pen to paper that lifts me and helps to focus my energy and thoughts.

—Susan Elaine Jenkins

Write with what gives you the most sensual satisfaction.

—Richard Hugo

Writing became such a process of discovery that I couldn't wait to get to work in the morning: I wanted to know what I was going to say.

—Sharon O'Brien

_____

_____

_____

_____

_____

_____

_____

_____

_____

_____

_____

_____

_____

_____

_____

_____

_____

_____

_____

_____

_____

Don't take criticism from someone you wouldn't go to for advice.

—Nat Russo

Writing is a voyage of discovery. The adventure is a metaphysical one... The writer lives between the upper and lower worlds: he takes the path in order to eventually become the path himself.

—Henry Miller

To care about words, to have a stake in what is written, to believe in the power of books—this overwhelms the rest, and beside it one's life becomes very small.

—Paul Auster

Poetry puts starch in your backbone so you can stand, so you can compose your life.

—Maya Angelou

Write what will stop your breath if you don't write.

—Grace Paley

Silence is a cage. These words are my wings.

—Jenim Dibie

Chapter 9

THE ROLE AND RESPONSIBILITY OF THE WRITER

Once your oxygen mask is firmly in place and your breath strong, your writing can sustain others. It can move them to action or be their remedy. Do not shirk from this duty. Remember that mighty pen? It's time to wield yours.

While art itself might not change the world, it's clear that it can empower those who will.

—Miguel Syjuco

Remember the world that writing opened for you as a child, awakening in you that sense of a larger universe, broader possibilities, the impulse to create? We need to remind ourselves that creation is important—it's not just something we do for ourselves; it gives life and energy to others.

—Sean W. Murphy

Something is always born of excess: great art was born of great terrors, great loneliness, great inhibitions, instabilities, and it always balances them.

—Anaïs Nin

Write to please just one person. If you open a window and make love to the world, so to speak, your story will get pneumonia.

—Kurt Vonnegut

_____

_____

_____

_____

_____

_____

_____

_____

_____

_____

_____

_____

_____

_____

_____

_____

_____

_____

_____

_____

_____

_____

_____

One of the functions of art is to give people the words to know their own experience... Storytelling is a tool for knowing who we are and what we want.

—Ursula le Guin

Remember that tiny projects are just as beautiful as big ones. Not everyone needs to write a three hundred-page memoir or five hundred-page epic fantasy novel. A very tiny writing project—like a love letter, short poem, or heartfelt card for a friend—can make a huge impact in someone's life. Tiny is a big deal.

—Alexandra Franzen

In the wholeheartedness of concentration, world and self begin to cohere. With that state comes an enlarging: of what may be known, what may be felt, what may be done.

—Jane Hirshfield

An absurd statement; how is a person going to write better or worse because he's thinking about who's going to read him?

—Jorge Luis Borges

Writing sometimes feels frivolous and sometimes sacred, but memory is one of my strongest muses. I serve her with my words. So long as people read, those we love survive however evanescently. As do we writers, saying with our life's work, Remember. Remember us. Remember me.

—Marge Piercy

Art is not what you see, but what you make others see.

—Edgar Degas

We are all in the gutter, but some of us are looking at the stars.

—Oscar Wilde

Good writing is about telling the truth. We are a species that needs and wants to understand who we are.

—Anne Lamott

Think of yourself as something much humbler and less spectacular, but far more interesting—a poet in whom live all the poets of the past, from whom all poets in time to come will spring. You have a touch of Chaucer in you, and something of Shakespeare; Dryden, Pope, Tennyson—to mention only the respectable among your ancestors—stir in your blood and sometimes move your pen a little to the right or to the left. In short you are an immensely ancient, complex, and continuous character, for which reason please treat yourself with respect.

—Virginia Woolf

The poet's, the writer's, duty is...to help man endure by lifting his heart.

—William Faulkner

Writing is also about a life engaged...community work, working in the schools or with grassroots conservation organizations is another critical component of my life as a writer. I cannot separate the writing life from a spiritual life, from a life as a teacher or activist or my life intertwined with family and the responsibilities we carry within our own homes. Writing is daring to feel what nurtures and breaks our hearts. Bearing witness is its own form of advocacy. It is a dance with pain and beauty.

—Terry Tempest Williams

I'm pursuing the craft of poetry not just for the sake of the craft itself but because I really believe in the power of language and stories to build bridges and create new possibilities.

—**José Olivarez**

When power corrupts, poetry cleanses.

—John F. Kennedy

Conclusion

ONWARD

For writers, until the final breath, there is no end. There is only the next word, the next thought, the next manuscript. It's a bit like having homework for the rest of your life, hopefully assignments you love. We'll never want for passion, or something to do.

I hope you find more joy than agony in writing and life. I wish I could meet each of you, hold your hand when things get tough, raise a cup when things go well. May the momentum you have gathered from filling these pages carry you onward through all of your days.

My best to you and yours,

NITA SWEENEY

About Nita Sweeney

 Nita Sweeney is the award-winning author of the memoir, *Depression Hates a Moving Target: How Running with My Dog Brought Me Back from the Brink.* Her personal essays and poems have been published in major magazines, books, newsletters, and blogs.

Nita earned a journalism degree from The E.W. Scripps School of Journalism at Ohio University, a law degree from The Ohio State University, and a Master of Fine Arts degree in creative writing from Goddard College. She studied with and assisted bestselling author Natalie Goldberg (*Writing Down the Bones*) for ten years and has taught writing and meditation to adult learners for two decades. She blogs about writing and life at *Bum Glue* and publishes the monthly writing newsletter, *Write Now Columbus.*

Nita lives in central Ohio with her husband (and biggest fan) Ed and their yellow Labrador retriever, Scarlet. For more information, visit her website nitasweeney.com or follow her on your favorite social media outlet.

About Brenda Knight

Brenda Knight began her career at HarperCollins, working with luminaries Paolo Coelho, Marianne Williamson, and Huston Smith. Knight was awarded IndieFab's Publisher of the Year award in 2014 at the American Library Association. Knight is the author of *Wild Women and Books*, *The Grateful Table*, *Be a Good in the World*, and *Women of the Beat Generation*, which won an American Book Award. Knight is a poet, writer, and editor. She also serves as president of the Women's National Book Association, San Francisco Chapter, and is an instructor at the annual San Francisco Writers Conference, Central Coast Writers Conference, and wherever she can be with fellow writers. She resides in San Francisco, CA.

Mango Publishing, established in 2014, publishes an eclectic list of books by diverse authors—both new and established voices—on topics ranging from business, personal growth, women's empowerment, LGBTQ studies, health, and spirituality to history, popular culture, time management, decluttering, lifestyle, mental wellness, aging, and sustainable living. We were recently named 2020's #1 fastest growing independent publisher by *Publishers Weekly*. Our success is driven by our main goal, which is to publish high quality books that will entertain readers as well as make a positive difference in their lives.

Our readers are our most important resource; we value your input, suggestions, and ideas. We'd love to hear from you—after all, we are publishing books for you!

Please stay in touch with us and follow us at:

Facebook: Mango Publishing
Twitter: @MangoPublishing
Instagram: @MangoPublishing
LinkedIn: Mango Publishing
Pinterest: Mango Publishing

Sign up for our newsletter at www.mangopublishinggroup.com and receive a free book!

Join us on Mango's journey to reinvent publishing, one book at a time.

CPSIA information can be obtained
at www.ICGtesting.com
Printed in the USA
JSHW021235290520
5969JS00001B/1

9 781642 502558